The Scream Within

The Scream Within

Mental Health and Clergy Marriages
Journey of a Pastor's Spouse

Reverend Benita L. Weathers, M.Div., MPH

GLORIOUS WORKS PUBLISHING
UPPER DARBY, PENNSYLVANIA

First Printing:2021

ISBN: 978-1-7335565-9-0

Glorious Works Publishing
201 Bywood Ave. #2214
Upper Darby, PA19082
www.gloriousworkspublishing.com

Special discounts are available on bulk purchases. For details, contact publisher at admin@gloriousworkspublishing.com.

Glorious Works Publishing can bring authors to your live events. For more information or to book an event, contact Glorious Works Publishing at admin@gloriousworkspublishing.com or visit our website at www.gloriousworkspublishing.com.

Publisher's Cataloging-In-Publication Data
(Prepared by The Donohue Group, Inc.)

Names: Weathers, Benita L., author.
Title: The scream within : mental health and clergy
    marriages : journey of a pastor's spouse /
    Reverend Benita L. Weathers, M.Div., MPH.
Description: Upper Darby, Pennsylvania : Glorious
    Works Publishing, [2021] | Includes
    bibliographical references.
Identifiers: ISBN 9781733556590
Subjects: LCSH: Weathers, Benita L.--Marriage. |
    Spouses of clergy--Biography. | Clergy--Mental
    health. | Depressed persons--Family relationships.
    | LCGFT: Autobiographies.
Classification: LCC BV4395 .W43 2021 | DDC 253.22--
    dc23

DEDICATION

I would like to dedicate this book to my husband, Rev. Dr. Wayne M. Weathers, for encouraging me to write from my perspective about our journey. Without his support and encouragement, it is likely this book would not have been written.

CONTENTS

ACKNOWLEDGMENTS

I want to acknowledge my children, Jasmine Nicole, James Matthew, and Kayla Nichelle, for continually encouraging me. In writing about the journey between their dad and me, they are very much a part of it, so their encouragement and support of me writing this means the world to me. I love them with every inch of my being!

INTRODUCTION

Depression in the General US Population

Major depression is defined as "a period of at least two weeks when a person experiences a depressed mood or loss of interest or pleasure in daily activities, and have a majority of specified symptoms, such as problems with sleep, eating, energy, concentration or self-worth."[1] Depression comes in many forms and impacts many people, not only those who suffer from it but those who care for them. It is one of the most common mental health disorders in the US and, for some, can be debilitating. In fact, depression is the leading cause of disability in the US among people ages 15-44 years, and it is projected that 1 in 5 Americans will be impacted by mental illness in their lifetime![2] Moreover, there are approximately $210.5 billion in lost earnings per year due to serious mental illness.[3]

Approximately 17.3 million adults in the US (7.1% of the entire adult population in the US) experienced at least one major episode of depression in 2017, and of those, 4.5% had severe

---

[1] https://www.nimh.nih.gov/health/statistics/major-depression.shtml, accessed 8/21/2019, 9:00 p.m.
[2] https://nndc.org/facts/?gclid=EAIaIQobChMItsHt0aCV5AIVhJ-zCh3_MgIpEAAYASAAEgIJdPD_BwE, accessed 8/21/2019, 9:45 p.m.
[3] IBID.

impairment as a result of their depression.[4] This may seem small in the grand scheme of things, but think about the fact that these statistics only represent documented accounts of depression. Think about those living with depression each day but keep it to themselves so as not to have folks "in their business." The actual number of people dealing with chronic depression is likely well over the 17.3 million reported. In fact, estimates suggest that only half of people with mental illness receive treatment.[5]

The Faith Community and Depression

Depression not only affects those in the general population, but it also affects those in faith communities, including pastors. A study conducted by the Clergy Health Initiative at Duke University Divinity School of more than 1700 United Methodist pastors in North Carolina found that the rate of depression among the clergy surveyed (11.1%) was double that of the national rate among the general population at the time (5.5%). Predictors of depression and anxiety among clergy include engaging in stressful activities such as grief counseling, competing demands of congregants, coupled with preparing sermons weekly under scrutiny. Moreover, many pastors, who often do quite a bit, feel guilty that they're not doing enough.[6]

Another study cited four essential ministry stressors, including personal criticism, boundary ambiguity, presumptive expectations, and family criticism.[7] On top of clergy feeling the pressure of having been called by God to do what they do, they also must endure the pressure of perceptions of the people whom they serve that they are "holy people without weaknesses." This holier than

---

[4] https://www.nimh.nih.gov/health/statistics/index.shtml, accessed 8/21/2019, 9:11 p.m.

[5] IBID.

[6] https://today.duke.edu/2013/08/clergydepressionnewsrelease, accessed 8/13/2019, 9:45 p.m.

[7] Proeschold-Bell, R. J., etal. Using effort-reward imbalance theory to understand high rates of depression and anxiety among clergy, J. Primary Prevention (2013) 34:439-453, pg. 440.

thou perception of clergy facilitates the belief that church leaders do not need as much support as others and preclude them from seeking help. Proeschold-Bell, et al., report that "some studies have found that clergy have relatively few confidants."[8]

Many strides have been made to assist those who suffer from depression to overcome it. In some cases, that means utilizing medications; in other cases, using therapy; and in many cases, both. While many people in our society have become comfortable with seeking the help and expertise of a therapist, this notion remains taboo among some in African American and faith communities. Notably, many people in African American church congregations view seeking mental health services not only as taboo but as having a lack of faith. However, when the one in the Christian faith community who seeks mental health services is the pastor- it's even more taboo.

For this reason, several pastors who have mental health challenges are left to their vices to deal with them. Studies have shown that many "African Americans rely on faith, spirituality, and religiosity to manage depressive symptoms, and are more likely to attend church and receive informal supports from church-based networks when experiencing distress."[9] But for the pastor, the reality is that he or she is not likely to confide in church members or even fellow clergy about their depression.

To Whom Can They Run?

So, where does the pastor who confronts depression run to when he or she needs help? Often, a pastor's first line of defense is his or her spouse. While some pastors' spouses may be trained counselors, most are not. So where does the spouse go, who is untrained, yet must take in all the issues affecting their loved one? Often, they go nowhere. They keep it all to themselves, grit and

---

[8] Bryant, K. et al. A rural African American faith community's solutions to depression disparities, Public Health Nursing, Vol. 31 (3): 262-271, 2013, pg. 263.
[9] IBID., 441.

bear it and just scream…within.

There is an enormous toll on the one who cares for a person dealing with depression, and when the depressed person is also high profile, it makes talking openly about it that much more difficult. As the caregiver, you want to make sure you don't say or do things that may trigger an episode of depression. You hold in your pain- the pain of watching the one you love in so much pain that they don't want to see the light of day, but most of all, the pain of not being able to say or do anything to alleviate that pain.

Depression Transference

Caregivers of individuals with depression often find themselves depressed. The loneliness, frustration, and pain associated with the depressed person can be transferred to the caregiver if they are not careful. Caregivers often feel the pain of the depressed person, at times so much that they begin to internalize the depression and become depressed themselves. But often, the caregiver can't afford to deal with depression in themselves because they need to remain stable for the depressed and, in some cases, the entire household.

Overcoming Fear

When I write this, it has been three years since the need to write this book was dropped in my spirit. For a long time, I did not want to write it. I did not want to think about the potential trigger it could be for my husband. I also did not want to appear to cast aspersion on him or embarrass him as he is, not only a pastor but a community leader. Fortunately, he is very open about dealing with depression and the fact that he sees a therapist. He has even been interviewed on radio programs and has written articles about being a pastor who has bouts of depression. Yet, I was still afraid even to tell him that I was thinking about writing this book.

Fast forward two years, and I finally got up the nerve to at least mention to him that I was thinking about writing a book about the impact of his depression on me. His response to me was, "Write the book. You have to write that book." My husband is always supportive of me and the many things that I do, preaching, teaching, working in my public health career, going back to school, etc. He is always super supportive. But I wasn't sure how he would receive my plans to write this book. As I began to write it, he looked at me in the eye and again affirmed, "You have to write this book. I may not be able to read it, but you must write it."

Purpose

The purpose of this book is to show other caregivers of persons dealing with depression, especially those in the church, that they are not alone. I hope that in reading this book, communities of mental health support will form in churches so that the scream within can become a scream without- without fear, without condemnation, without ridicule, without embarrassment. I hope that by sharing my experience as the spouse of a pastor who is challenged by depression, others who deal with similar challenges will find hope and support.

1 THE SCREAM WITHIN

My Lens

Before jumping into my journey as a married woman and pastor's spouse caring for a husband who copes with depression, I want to provide you with some context on the lens through which I first came to view depression. I grew up the youngest child of a pastor. My entire life was spent in church, learning about God and my relationship with Him. We went to church from what felt like sun up to sun down every Sunday and sometimes mid-week. From a very young age, I was always taught to trust God with everything- challenges big, small, and everything in-between. As the youngest in my family, I was shielded from serious challenges, thanks largely to my parents and siblings.

As a young child, I had a happy life. We were by no means well off but still fortunate to travel and see other parts of the United States of America and be exposed to different cultures. I have always been a "happy-go-lucky" person and tried to find the good in every situation, regardless of how awful it might have been. My family often reminisces, even now, of how I was such a happy baby- always smiling. I like the feeling of being happy and have tried to find it even when it seemed nearly impossible to be found. That said, I never really had any personal experience with depression, at least not knowingly. Like any other family, we had our ups and downs, and everything was not always peaches and cream, but in general, we were happy as a family.

Growing up, I never heard anyone talk about depression. I did not know the varying levels of depression. My view of depression was the occasional, temporary bout of sadness in which one might find him or herself. However, I would later find out that this was not depression at all. I also did not see many tears shed among my family members. To this day, I have only witnessed my mom cry once or twice. I don't ever recall my dad crying or seeming low. Everyone just seemed to go on with life and handle whatever life gave without much complaint- we rolled with the punches and got back up! None of this is to say that no one in my family dealt with depression. It's to say that if anyone did suffer from depression, it did not show, and no one spoke about it. This is the lens through which I viewed depression.

Needless to say, my lens was cloudy. I didn't know what it looked like or how it presented itself. I didn't know if it was constant or sporadic; if it only showed itself as sadness or overt pain; if it showed up as anguish- I just didn't know. My family was known for having many discussion topics around the family dinner table, but depression was not one of them. I certainly never heard of my father or any of his ministerial colleagues seeing a therapist, even though, as clergy, they provided therapy in the form of spiritual counseling to others all the time.

The one thing I did know was there was no such thing as seeing a therapist- that was for people with serious mental problems, and people with issues that severe were institutionalized. People in the church didn't need it. They had God, and that was enough. If God wasn't enough, they needed to check their faith. Otherwise, when challenges arose that caused distress, no matter how severe, you'd just pray about it and "get over it." We never discussed that sometimes even those of great faith need help to get over it. They need tools to help them get through their challenges, and that's ok. We didn't discuss that just because someone sees a therapist doesn't mean that they're crazy; rather, they're in-tune enough with themselves to admit when they need help.

I have always been one to desire to understand people's behaviors. Even as a young child or teenager, when people did things that upset me, rather than get angry with them, I desired to know where the behavior was coming from. I understood on some fundamental level that people's actions, good and bad, are steeped in their personal histories. And even though I may not have understood the reasoning for the behavior, I desired to understand and empathize. I would often think to myself, *I'm not particularly fond of their behavior, but I know it's coming from a deep place, and I hope they can get healing from their pain.*

I also understood on some level that negative behaviors were the manifestation of screams within that needed a way out but were trapped- trapped by secrecy, shame, fear, etc. Screams within are like mice in a maze, bumping into walls under the anxiety of feeling trapped while their acute sense of smell allows them to know that if they can just find their way out of the maze, there's a treat waiting at the end and the scream could be turned inside out.

A New Lens

I realize that the lens through which I saw depression as a child growing up in the 1970s and '80s was no different from how most people saw it then. Unlike now, particularly in the black community, it was not a point of discussion. This view also stems from the history of African Americans as a people, forced to survive the brutal physical and mental torment of a system created to crush us. Our ancestors and elders simply did not have the time nor privilege to be depressed, let alone seek help for it.

However, today is a new day, and it's not until you see depression up close and personal that you begin to realize its depth. As a child, depression was like a shallow pool where I could stand up and not be afraid of drowning, but as an adult, witnessing it up close, it was more like a deep ocean with currents that pulled you under without warning. As a young woman on the verge of becoming a newly-wed, little did I know that the lens through which I viewed depression was about to change drastically, and it would take me by storm in an ocean of loneliness.

Silence and Loneliness

Depression is not only lonely for the individual dealing with it but also for those who care about them. The loneliness is amplified when the depression is undiagnosed, and there seems to be no rhyme or reason to a person's actions. During the early years of our marriage, I noticed certain behaviors that I did not understand. Rather than confront my husband about them, I sat in silence and loneliness. I loathed and still despise confrontation, so if it felt like inquiring about an action would lead to conflict, I just remained silent. As I stated earlier, I knew the behavior was from a history to which I had not yet been privy to learn. We had no family in North Carolina, where we lived, and our oldest daughter was an infant at the time. Rather than confront whatever was going on with my husband, mood swings, and sometimes profound sadness, I left it alone and put all my energy into my baby girl. I would cling to her like a little girl with a doll that brought her comfort in times of turmoil and confusion. Clinging to her seemed to bring me life during the fragile and challenging aspects of my life at that time. She was my life raft in a turbulent ocean.

The silence and loneliness did not only occur at home when it was just our baby and me. I could be surrounded by people and feel a sense of loneliness.   I could have a smile on my face and happily interact with those around me and still feel like the only one in the room. My mind was always preoccupied with what I could do to make him happy. What I didn't realize at that age and as a newly-wed was that an internally unhappy person could not be *made* happy. In other words, one's external environment does not dictate one's happiness. Happiness must come from within. But one who is depressed is, by definition, unhappy. Depression is defined as a pressing down or lowering; a state of feeling sad, dejection, anger, and anxiety; feelings of dejection and hopelessness (Merriam-Webster Dictionary for iPhone, 2019). No matter what went on around me, I felt like I had to figure out how to lift him out of this constant state of unhappiness, and I also felt that there was no one out there who could understand what I was going through and how it made me feel- like a failure. The burden was far too heavy for me to lift alone, yet I felt the need to do just that- work it out by myself and scream…within.

The thing about screaming within is that the screams echo and vibrate throughout every facet of one's life. Inward screams have no outlet and, therefore, no release. When a person continues to hold in those cries that they so desperately need to release, the inward screams' vibrations cause internal destruction- mentally, spiritually, and sometimes in ways that manifest physically. During these times, I longed for a safe space to vent and let go of the pain and frustration I was feeling within. But where would I go?

Who Can I Run To?

There were times that I wished I had someone in whom to confide about this. But who was there? I was raised, like most African-Americans, to keep my business at home. What happens at home stays at home. I didn't speak with my family because I didn't want to cause them concern. I didn't have any close friends nearby, and even if I did, I would not have spoken with them about it. As a newlywed, in particular, I was not going to my *in-loves* (this is what we call in-laws in our family) about it. There was no one to whom I could turn for understanding, solace, encouragement, or strength; therefore, I did the only thing I knew how to do in this situation- I prayed. I asked God to give me an understanding of the internal turmoil that was happening in one whom I loved so dearly. I prayed that my husband could see in himself what I saw- one who was loving, supportive, and talented with a brilliant mind. I prayed that he would soon be able to deal with whatever was causing him to be in so much pain. I prayed that I would be his strength and help him through it all.

As a woman, and particularly as an African-American woman, I believed that I was supposed to be invincible through it all and raise him out of this misery. I needed to be the wife who made him feel like the strong man he already was. I needed to be the confidant who kept all his secrets and made him feel safe. I needed to be the therapist (albeit untrained) to hear all his deepest woes and past life events that hurt him deeply. I needed to *make* him happy. But nothing I had said or done sufficed. As a young wife and mother, I felt like I was failing him somehow, and by extension, failing our family. I couldn't figure out what I was doing wrong, but I also did not feel comfortable talking about it to anyone.

Since I did not have an outlet, I was left to the devices of my mind. As a very young child, whenever I found myself in an unpleasant space, I would retreat into the recesses of my mind. I would go to a happy place and find solace there. I would imagine I was in a happy place, with happy people, doing happy things. Even as an adult, when I felt depressed or in a situation that brought me low, rather than use drugs or drink alcohol, I would chew gum and go into my mind to another place where I felt happy. However, one cannot remain in a fictitious world- the real world awaits, and one needs to know how to *live* in his or her reality. In the real world, there is no such thing as constant happiness. We must figure out how to balance the good times with the bad.

A part of being adept at the balancing act of facing all that life brings is not running from the bad. I have learned that in confronting negative experiences, I can discover more about myself and the world surrounding me. When we face difficult situations, we learn that we can be resilient and move through the pain, not running a sprint but at the steady pace of a long-distance race. Our muscles might hurt, but they will be strengthened; our bodies will bend, but they will not break, our minds will develop the propensity to think positively through it all.

Is this Personal?

While I struggled with not feeling as though I had an "earthly or real-world" outlet, I also grappled with taking things personally. There were times that the source of my husband's frustration, sadness, or anger wasn't clear to me, and watching him experience these moods while feeling helpless to assist made me think it was my fault. I had no clue what was happening with him internally, so I took things personally that had nothing to do with me; instead, they had everything to do with the inner demons that he needed to fight. But because there was no one else around on whom to put the blame, I blamed myself.

Whenever that elephant was in the room, I just let it remain and hover until it decided to leave the room on its own. I didn't talk about it. I didn't ask questions. I didn't scream or shout. I just didn't. Taking things personally did not do any good for my self-esteem as a wife. My reasons for not engaging in dialogue with my husband about how I was feeling were two-fold: On the one hand, I thought, what if he truly did see me as the impetus of how he felt in any given moment? Talking about it might cause conflict, and I needed to stay far away from that; and on the other hand, I felt his knowing that I often took things personally would make him more depressed because the last thing he would ever want to do is hurt me in any way. So, the elephant remained until that bout of depression concluded, and life moved along as usual…until the next one.

There didn't seem to be consistency in the rate at which the "next one" would come. It could be days, weeks, or mere minutes. It was challenging to understand the triggers to the depression, which is another reason I frequently viewed myself as the trigger. I thought something I had said or done made my husband go into a depression. Therefore, I always tried to be careful about what I said, when I'd say it and how I'd say it. For me, it was personal because nothing else made sense. I didn't understand what was going on, and in those moments when I was alone, I'd go into my room, into my shell, and cry. Besides praying, which I did often, crying was the only other thing I could do to, in some way, release my pain. Of course, I could not cry in front of my husband or children. I needed to be strong for them. I never wanted even to look like I had been weeping.

There were times when someone would notice that my eyes were red and watery and would ask if I was crying. The answer went something like, "No, my allergies are acting up" or "No, I think I'm catching a cold," or something like that. At some point amid the tears, I thought, *There's something at the root of this issue, but what? Moreover, how can the problem be pulled at the root? What is the weed-killer that can dispose of the issue? For the scream within to become a scream without,* I needed to define it. What exactly was it?

2 DEFINING THE SCREAM

What is Really Happening Here?

For the first few years of marriage, I pondered, wondered, prayed about what was going on with my husband. Don't get me wrong, these struggles weren't constant, but they were enough that it made me feel as if there had to be more to the depressive bouts than what could be seen at the surface level. There was some deep-rooted pain inside, but what was it, and where did it come from? I prayed, often about these things, but mostly about how to make the pain stop. I saw a strong, brilliant man with various gifts and talents that could take him wherever he so desired. He was a drummer, a playwright, a poet, a song-writer, a hip-hop artist, one who has a knack for thinking profoundly and providing deep insight about various topics. He was also a masterful preacher and teacher. I could see all of this in him so clearly, yet he could not see any of these characteristics in himself. Where others would use charm and swagger to BS (*yes, I said BS*) their way through life, he had integrity and chose not to forfeit that for the things the world tends to desire. Still, he did not see these qualities in himself. *Why can't he see in himself what I see, what God sees?*

When we were cultivating a friendship before marriage, we would talk on the phone, literally for hours, about everything from politics to religion to Scooby-Doo and everything in-between! This was my initial attraction to him. When we first met, I had just gotten out of a relationship and vowed that I was done; finished with relationships. I expressed to him early on that I had no desire for a romantic relationship. Moreover, I was in the process of applying to graduate school out of town, and while I did not yet know where I was going, I knew it would be outside of Baltimore. Therefore, it was pointless to start a new relationship knowing that I would be leaving in just a few months.

On top of that, I met him in a way that was similar to how I met the guy I dated previously- at an event sponsored by members of Delta Sigma Theta Sorority, Inc. As a woman of Alpha Kappa Alpha Sorority, Inc., I felt perhaps it was taboo for me to meet another man at a Delta function (just kidding for my Delta friends who might be reading this book)☺. But the more we talked, the more we connected. I was especially captivated by the fact that he respected my desire not to want a romantic relationship. He never tried to push himself on me. He gave me space; he even helped me get through the pain of my previous relationship, and then it happened. I supported him by seeing a play that he had written, produced, and starred in where he was wearing a vest with no shirt underneath in one scene. When I saw those guns (muscular arms for those unfamiliar with this vernacular ☺)- that was it! Fast forward a few months, I found myself singing and relating to a song by Deborah Cox that had come out several months prior, "Nobody's Supposed to be Here!" In the song, she sings, *"How did you get here? Nobody's supposed to be here. I tried that love thing for the last time!"* That's where I was in my life- no desire for another relationship gone wrong; no desire to be in-love- I tried that love thing for the last time...or so I thought.

As our friendship developed into a romantic relationship, we remained, and still remain best friends. One thing that keeps our marriage so healthy is the ability to converse about any and everything under the sun. I could talk to him openly and freely like one of the girls, and he could speak to me freely as with one of the fellas. As time progressed, he began to open up to me about many things- things he never talked about with anyone else. As I stated earlier, I'm no trained therapist (yet), but I knew that what he was experiencing was far more than I could assist him with. Yes, I was a listening ear, and I cared to listen, but this was something that required more than a listening ear. It required someone who knew how to delve into the deepest recesses of the mind and get to the root of the problem. As difficult as it was, about three years into the marriage, I had to finally ask the question, "Have you ever thought about seeing a therapist?" I finally reached that point when I realized certain pain-points in his life that he repeated often and similar themes that frequently emerged during our conversations.

Stigma

Of course, seeing a therapist never entered his mind because he thought, like most African-Americans, seeing a therapist is equated with being crazy. He did not want to be stigmatized and wasn't thrilled about the notion of telling a stranger his business. On top of that, he had just become a first-time pastor. He did not want to seek therapy and risk church members finding out. Given the stigma of mental illness within the church, he could not risk the embarrassment this might cause the church and our family.

Stigma is defined in the Merriam-Webster Dictionary as "a mark of shame or discredit[10]." It might also be described as a feeling of shame or judgment from someone else. These feelings of guilt are the very things that keep individuals in mental bondage. We often concern ourselves more with what others think about us rather than freeing ourselves to think positively of ourselves regardless of what others think. Many of us have been conditioned this way. Stigma is like a ball and chain around the neck of someone. Too often, individuals become accustomed to the bondage and, therefore, don't try to find the key to unlock the

---

[10] Merriam-Webster Dictionary for Iphone, 2019.

chain. Sometimes the fear of freedom causes one to remain in the bondage of stigma because freedom can only come by exposing the pain and confronting it head-on.

As one who is deftly afraid of confrontation, I understand how paralyzing it can be to stand toe-to-toe with a giant. The Christian faith teaches us that we can do all things through Christ who strengthens us and that we are more than conquerors in Jesus. But we must grow to a point where we trust that when we sling the rock, God will kill the giant. For some, depression is a giant, and many who suffer from it are afraid to sling the rock. Why? Because slinging the rock means bringing those things in the deepest, most remote, and dark areas of the mind out to the light. It requires exposing some distressing memories or situations. To *expose* means to uncover, reveal, lay bare, show, display, exhibit, manifest, unveil, unmask, **leave unprotected**- this is scary, so the rock stays in hand, and the giant shouts victory!

For several years, my husband tried to handle things independently, but they weren't getting any better. The thing about depression is that it not only affects the person with the disease; it affects those around him or her, particularly those in his or her inner circle, i.e., spouses, children, other close family members, and friends. There can be an entire army of people, all afraid of the giant- never thinking that if they combine forces, they can slay the giant together. There's also the notion that the depressed person doesn't want to "drag" their loved ones into their melodrama. For one dealing with the challenges of depression, it might appear that they are helping their family members and loved ones by keeping them at bay and trying to handle it all alone. But the fact of the matter is that depression is not only verbal. Those who genuinely love and know them can **feel** it, even when the depressed individual tries his or her best to hide it. And the **feeling** is a heavy weight felt by all in its presence. At some point, I believe that my husband began seeing the impact his depression was having on me and our children. Thus, he made a courageous move to seek therapy.

Finding the Right Fit

By this time, we had moved to a new city, and he was pastoring his second congregation. Although he was finally ready to take that first step to heal, it was not an easy decision. He had to factor in that he was a new pastor in the city, and there was still concern about the stigma attached to mental illness. Additionally, finding a therapist who also had the spiritual foundation to incorporate with the medical would be challenging. He did not want someone whose only approach to healing his mind would be to medicate him. He wanted someone who could also relate to, respect, and believe in his faith.

As he began to search for a therapist that fit the characteristics he desired, not only did my husband find a therapist who was a Christian, but he found one who was also a pastor. Being a pastor can be a very stressful calling in and of itself, but coupled with depression, it can be that much more challenging. As a pastor, it is sometimes difficult to show vulnerability to those whom you serve, one because they look to you for strength amid all kinds of circumstances, and two, because they need to see you as a leader. The leadership of a pastor with known depression might be questioned and thus undermined. Having a therapist who was also personally familiar with pastoring's struggles and challenges was a significant help.

Making a decision to seek mental health care and finding the right fit in a therapist, however, is only half the battle. Depression doesn't stop or even lessen based on these factors alone. One never really knows how much therapy will be required to make progress nor the timetable within which healing will begin. The road to seeing the benefits of counseling could be short or long, depending on the individual's backstory and the amount of repressed pain compounded over the years that a therapist would need to peel back. Meanwhile, life moves on. While seeking therapy, my husband still needed to function in his roles as husband, father, pastor, son, etc. Conversely, we still needed to serve in our roles for him- wife and children. He needed our support and encouragement to fight through his pain, along with the aid of his therapist.

Of course, as his wife, I knew that he would start seeing a therapist; however, it was not something he wanted our children to know. He did not want them to be embarrassed or think badly of him for having to seek therapy. Our children were young at the time, so he felt it would be pretty easy to conceal from them that he was in therapy. One day when he was scheduled to see the therapist, the children were home from school, and I was at work. They were too young to leave home alone, and he desperately needed to see the therapist. He did not want to cancel the appointment, so he decided to take the children with him. He told them that he had a doctor's appointment and that they would need to go with him. He also had a talk with them about being good as they waited in the waiting room while he was in with the "doctor." All was well. The children sat patiently in the waiting room while he saw the therapist. He came out of the therapist's office, gathered up the kids, and they all walked to the car. When they got in the car, my son, who was around eight or nine years old at the time, looked at my husband and asked, "Why do you need to see a therapist?"

Revelation

At this point, my husband realized it was time to move through the stigma associated with depression and come clean- to our children and the world. He began to open up to the children about his depression, mood swings, and inability to sometimes be mentally present with us. He conducted radio interviews and wrote articles about his experience being a pastor who was challenged with depression. But even with this progress being made, the road to healing would still be a long one. Bouts of depression would still occur, mood swings, emotional ebbs and flows- everything that comes with depression. More than anything, he needed his family to be there for him and support him as he walked through and tried to overcome this challenge. Someone would need to care for him, and that someone would be me.

Even though my husband had settled in on the idea of having a therapist, he still needed that ear and voice of reason at home. After all, therapy sessions are usually no more than an hour at a time and, depending on one's insurance coverage, those times can be few and far between. In the interim, a person dealing with depression needs a safe space to be him or herself and get things off their chest that might otherwise yield another bout of depression. Pastors undergo an enormous amount of pressure to be perfect humans who are always there for their parishioners. Most parishioners, however, don't comprehend a pastor's life: concern for church members; responsibility for their souls; being present for them. All of this pressure, some of which is self-inflicted, can be difficult for the average person to handle. For a person who suffers from depression and anxiety, however, the pressure can feel ten times heavier.

While the average parishioner does not understand what being a pastor entails, the pastor's spouse has a front-row seat. This is the person with whom the pastor bounces ideas, voices anger regarding things that might happen with parishioners, seeks advice about handling delicate situations best, navigates relationships with others in the church, etc. The pastor's spouse becomes the sounding board for relatively everything, especially those situations that are heavy and a hard load to carry.

3 BEING THE SOUNDING BOARD

When the Listening Ear Becomes a Sounding Board

A sounding board is a structure behind or over a pulpit, rostrum, or platform to give distinctness and sonority to sound. Figuratively, it is a person or group on whom one tries out an idea or opinion as a means of evaluating it.[11] The origin of the term sounding board stems from the Renaissance Era. In order for the preacher's voice to be heard throughout the farthest reaches of the church building, a flat wooden canopy would be placed over the pulpit to amplify the sound[12].   I mentioned earlier that prior to my husband starting therapy and then in between his therapy sessions, I was the one on whom he would bounce thoughts, ideas, pain, anguish, etc. I was his sounding board, which is not unusual among married couples. They should be that for one another. Problematically, in some instances, the sound of his release of anguish and frustration was a relief for him but distress for me.

The way a literal sounding board works is that the sound waves of the one speaking bounce off the sounding board and then outward such that the sound is projected. There were times, however, when the sounds wouldn't bounce. Instead, they drove

---

Merriam-Webster Dictionary for Iphone, 2019.
Phone, 2018.
[12] https://www.merriam-webster.com/dictionary/sounding%20board#note-1

into me, and I kept them there. In other words, I absorbed his agony over and over again. I don't regret being his sounding board. As his other half, I am happy to provide him with the listening ear we all need from time to time. The problem is that as my listening ear became a sounding board, the vibrations would sometimes shake my very foundation, and rather than the sound echoing outward, it would remain trapped and would shake me inwardly.

I began to internalize everything that he "got off his chest" and everything that "pissed him off." After all, this is what spouses should do for each other, right? The "each other" part is where I was lacking. I tend to keep things inside. When I am bothered or frustrated, I pray, take a few deep breaths, and keep it moving. However, at some point, the sound waves build up internally, and with no outlet, one is bound to implode or explode. As one who keeps things bottled up inside, my frustration would show itself sometimes as crying; other times as a distant stare or going into a room alone, pacing back and forth trying to figure out how to get the scream out. For the most part, however, the scream remained trapped within, creating anxiety and tension.

Full of It

As I internalized much of his anguish, I neglected to deal with my own. As I stated earlier in the book, being a pastor is not easy, and being the pastor's spouse is equally as arduous. It requires a lot of balancing- church, work, household, dealing with personalities, and sometimes, conflict. As a PK, I was determined to also protect my children from the expectations heaped upon pastors' kids. I began to fill up with my husband's stuff, the kids' stuff, my stuff. I sometimes felt like I was bursting at the seams. Everyone else's issues stuck with me, and I felt like I had no outlet to deal with my problems. My number one priority is making sure that my family is ok. Like a lot of women, I neglected my own mental and spiritual needs.

I needed someone to be a sounding board for me. But who?

My husband already had enough issues to deal with as a pastor and one who was challenged with depression. I felt like talking to him about my distress would in some way cause him to despair more, and therefore, be in more pain leading to more depression. I could not bear to do this to him, so I kept a lot inside. I have a very close relationship with my sister and brothers, but they too had their own issues with which to contend. Moreover, I did not want them to think that they needed to run to my rescue. As the youngest child, I was often protected and sheltered. It's one of the reasons I decided to go 600+ miles away from home to attend college. I needed to prove to myself that I could survive on my own, solve my own problems, make my own decisions, and handle the consequences of them, both good and bad.

I had friends that I may have been able to talk to, but many would not understand the life of a pastor and his or her family. Pastors and their families tend to be guarded because the expectation is for them to keep up pseudo appearances of being perfect. All pastors' families should look like the one on the church fan where everyone is poised, polished, and near perfect. The fact of the matter, however, is that pastors' families are imperfect like all other families. In fact, the pressure to be near perfect often drives these families to be worse off than others. I can remember as a child sometimes wishing that my dad was not a pastor, wishing he had chosen a typical career before I understood that his career was a calling. I didn't speak to others because I didn't think they would understand, and I also didn't want to lay the weight of my issues on them. So, there I was, filling up and becoming constipated with other people's stuff...and mine too.

Implosion

People often come to me for advice or just a listening ear. I enjoy listening to others and being a safe space for them to have an outlet to vent their frustrations or work through their issues. I had done this for many years and never felt bothered when others came to me. I never really felt the impact, so I didn't think that taking in other peoples' issues impacted me. My sister would often worry about me and ask me the question, "Where do you go to vent?" To which I would respond, "I don't." I give it to God, and that's it. While I do believe what it says in 1 Peter 5:7, to cast our cares on [Jesus] because he cares for us[13], I also believe that God allows human interaction to cast our cares. I thought I was handling it all well until…the outward implosion.

One day, I had lunch with a dear friend who also happens to be a pastor's wife and minister. She was a God-send because, finally, someone could relate to some of the very issues that I dealt with. We met, as we occasionally did, purchased our lunch, found a table, and began to catch up with each other as we had not seen or spoken with each other in a bit. We smiled and laughed, catching up on all the stories about our children and how they were managing life as adults. We talked about our jobs and how we were getting along balancing full-time employment with church, ministry, and home duties.

I'm not sure what happened or what we were even talking about at the moment, but all of a sudden, in a room full of strangers, I began to cry profusely. I don't even know what triggered it, but I completely lost control. I literally started bawling. It was at that moment that I realized I was having a mental meltdown. I could not stop crying. She came over to my side of the table to console me. Had it been anyone else, I would have been very embarrassed, but I knew she felt my pain. She suggested that I use my health benefits and get some counseling.

Therapy

I took her suggestion and utilized the benefits to get counseling. As I set off to my first counseling session, I couldn't help but think, what if this counselor knows of my husband or knows someone who knows of him? What if she mentions to someone that Pastor Weathers's wife is in therapy with her? Of

---

[13] Holy Bible, NKJV.

course, I knew that legally, she is supposed to follow the rules of confidentiality, but what if…? I was mainly concerned because the practice was located in the community where we live, and what if one of my neighbors saw me going into or coming out of the therapist's office? As all of this raced through my head, I began to hesitate about seeking counseling for myself. What a hypocrite- as much as I encouraged my husband and others to seek therapy to assist them with some of life's challenges, here I doubted and seriously considered backing out.

Moving Ahead

I didn't back out. At least, not at first. I decided to push forward and give it a try. I never told anyone in my family that I was going to see a therapist. I didn't want them to worry about me, and I still wanted to protect them, so I kept that secret buried deep. When I arrived at the first session, I was very nervous. I had always been able to provide therapy for myself, or so I thought. The idea of sharing what I was going through with a stranger was mind-boggling to me, even though, as I said before, I often suggested this very thing to others. Furthermore, I wasn't even sure that I could articulate my feelings in a way that would make sense.

The first session was more or less an introduction. The therapist introduced herself and explained her process, completed some paperwork, and she started to try to get to know a little about me. However, I noticed that she did most of the talking! I could barely get a word in. I thought to myself, "I thought this was supposed to be about me- an opportunity for me to express what I was going through!" I left the first session feeling like I had wasted my time. I didn't expect to be healed through one session, but I thought that I would release some of my frustration. Although that didn't happen, I decided to give it another try. I scheduled a second session the following week.

As I prepared to attend the next session, I went with an open mind. I tried not to be negative based on the outcome or lack thereof of the first session. When I entered the therapist's office, I sat in the chair where I felt most comfortable and prepared to have an opportunity to scream. It didn't happen. In fact, the second session felt much like the first. The therapist did a lot of talking, and I remained frustrated. As they say, "I gave it the old college try," but at that point, I was done with counseling. I was already in a much better headspace than the weeks prior, and I decided to make session two my last session, at least with that therapist. Oh well, so much for me having a sounding board. I am not discounting seeking therapy later, but for now, it would remain God and me.

4 CRACKING THE EGGS AND WALKING ON THE SHELLS

Walking on Eggshells

Depression often causes anxiety and uncertainty about what to expect from a person who is depressed. What kind of mood will they be in? What will I walk into when I get home? It's a lot like cracking eggs and walking on the shells. You know how it is if an egg, or a glass for that matter, falls on the kitchen floor, and you tiptoe around it to keep from stepping on something that might cut or cause severe pain? This is what it's like when you care for someone who battles depression. You do all that you can to try not to say or do something that might cause the individual pain or trigger an episode of depression.

There were many times on my commute home from work or school or wherever that I wondered what might be awaiting me when I arrived home. I would become filled with anxiety. My heart would race. My breathing would be short and labored at the thought of what I might find when I arrived home. Sometimes, I would come home to find my husband in a great mood, smiling and joking. Other times I was greeted by questions from my children, "What's wrong with dad?" "Did something happen to dad?" "Why is dad angry?"

In those moments, I felt it necessary to go into survival mode and, beyond everything else, to protect my children. During those times, my husband would usually be tucked away in our room or the basement, or he would step out of the house so as not to "bring down the mood" in the place. I would try to keep the kids occupied and focused on something other than what's wrong with dad. We would play games or watch a movie or do some other activity. It was amazing how I could distract them and shift their thoughts elsewhere, but I could not do that for myself. I did an excellent job of hiding my anxiety from the children so they could have some peace. When bedtime rolled around, we would do our customary circle prayer, after which I went to each of their rooms, tucked them in, and sang, "Jesus Loves Me." Lights out.

Darkness

When the lights went out for the kids, they seemed to go out for me too. You see, just as much as I was an intentional distraction for them so they wouldn't be focused on their dad's depression, they were a distraction for me too. One way that I coped with my husband's depression was to lose myself in our children. But when they went to bed, there I was, left alone to deal with it myself. In those moments, I felt so alone- like a distant star on a dark night whose light was eclipsed. The kids would be in bed, my husband would be somewhere in the house depressed, and I would be somewhere in the house screaming...within.

When the episodes of depression hit, most times, after sorting through it himself, my husband would discuss with me whatever triggered the episode. There was no specific time frame within which he felt like he could talk about it. Sometimes it would be hours, other times days. But during the lull, the space in between finding out what was wrong and not knowing, I found myself in a state of anxiety- my heart racing, hands shaking, worried about whether he would pull through it this time, worried about whether the kids would pull through this time, worried about whether I would pull through this time.

Losing Myself to Gain Myself

After several years, I ended up returning to school to work on a Master of Divinity degree. While I knew full well that God was calling me to further my education and go deeper into ministry, I also found it to be a way to lose myself. Let me explain. I was working full time, attending school part-time and studying, doing homework and papers the rest of the time. Therefore, I had no time to focus on my husband's depression. I simply, literally, did not have the time. It was a great escape. I lost myself in my studies and gained myself at the same time.

I was able to gain myself because before, it was all about what was going on with my husband and our children. On some level, it was wonderful just focusing on something that I enjoyed, something that would be my escape from one reality and shaped into a new reality. My weeks consisted of working 8-hour days, attending class 2-3 days per week from 7-10 p.m., then driving an hour back home. On the days I didn't have class, I was up until 1, 2, or 3 a.m. doing homework, writing papers, and studying. As you can see, when I say I had no time to focus on my husband's depression, I literally had no time.

Feeling Guilty for Finding Me

But as I was losing myself in all of my work, I felt like I was being unfair to our children and my husband. I thought that I wasn't providing them with the time I should have and wasn't protecting them. After all, the children were too young to fend for themselves during a bout of depression. Before, they had me to shield them in some ways. Now they didn't. I felt I left them abandoned to deal with something for which they were too young to handle.

I constantly fought guilt about doing what I was called to do and passionate about at their expense. I especially felt shame when I learned that my youngest daughter would fall asleep in our TV room and not go to bed until she knew I was home. It wasn't until later that I would realize that seminary was a form of therapy for me. It allowed me to escape my every day and reconnect with

God and myself. It was my outlet, my scream…without.

Am I Helping or Enabling?

Throughout this journey, I found myself being silent about many things so as not to be the impetus of my husband's episodes of depression. I would often not voice opposition for fear of causing an argument. My fear of arguing was two-fold: 1) as a child, I witnessed several disputes between various people, and none of them ended well. I never saw progress come as a result of arguing, only distance and more anger. This was something I did not want in my marriage, so I avoided it at all costs. I am fortunate that my husband and I have the type of relationship where we can discuss our disagreements and, in the end, grow from them. However, when we were first married, I was not as confident voicing opposition because I thought, based on previous experiences, that it would ultimately lead to our demise as a couple, so I remained silent. 2) I feared that my opposition would lead to a bout of depression for my husband- another thing that I wanted to avoid at all costs.

But as time progressed, I began to wonder, am I helping or enabling? Enabling means to make possible, practical, or easy.[14] Was trying to avoid the "elephant in the room" the best course of action? Would avoidance of an issue make it such that the depression would lessen? Was I making it easy to use depression as a cop-out for dealing with problems rather than facing them head-on? I found myself saying things in my head that probably should have been spoken aloud. It would probably have been more helpful to my husband and me to face certain things head-on, rather than doing what I thought would make it so the depression would lessen or go away. I found that not only did my silence not help my husband's depression, but it caused me to hold in more than I could bear, leading to more and more inward screams. I realized that I had mastered the art of masking my emotions and holding them in to save face. But whose face does

---

[14] Merriam-Webster Dictionary Application for iPhone, 2018.

it truly save? No one's. It's best to face things head-on and deal with them than to internalize them to the point that you cause yourself mental or physical harm.

Cracking the Egg

Although walking on eggshells or biting into that random shell that slipped into the egg while cooking can cause pain, the egg must be cracked to get to the nourishment at the center of it. An egg has a tough yet fragile exterior. It remains strong until you drop it. When you boil it, the shell becomes even stronger. You can dye it and paint it and make it beautiful on the outside, but you will never benefit from its nutrients until you crack it. Writing this book for me is cracking the egg. Moving past the mask that I've created externally and allowing myself to be cracked, not to be hurt, but to get to the nutrients on the inside by screaming aloud and penning these pages will hopefully liberate someone else.

What makes this leg of the journey more difficult is that cracking the egg for me involves sharing, not only about me but my other half as well. As I mentioned earlier, it took me two years to share with my husband that I was even considering writing this book. But once I found the courage to crack the egg of informing him of my thoughts, I was able to benefit from the nutrients of his encouragement to write it. When he said to me, "You have to write the book. I may not be able to read it, but you have to write it," I no longer felt the need to tiptoe through the broken shells because what mattered most were the nutrients I found at the center of his courage and encouragement.

5 I NEED YOU TO SEE ME

Removing the Mask

As one who likes to portray a positive image at all times, I tend to smile even when I want to cry, laugh when I want to shout, behave politely even when I want to smash something or someone! But there are times when I just wish that others could truly see me. I don't think I knew I felt this way until one day when a church member gave me a card that said, "I just want you to know that I *see* you." I immediately began to cry because whether I thought about it or not, it made me feel good that someone took the time to notice me. It was as if she saw behind the smile, my mask, and saw the real me. One who was broken but being held together by Scotch tape- you know- the kind you can't see, supposedly, but it's there, holding the pieces together.

It occurred to me that I had become so accustomed to seeing others, I never gave a second thought to a desire to have others see me. It wasn't until that moment that I realized how important it was to have others take note of when I need comfort. It was something that I never sought because it was always more important for me to be present for my family and others than to be present for myself.

Prior to my husband organizing the church where we are now,

he was the pastor of an older, established church. Before his resignation, the church underwent severe turmoil that devastated our family. The pain that it caused cut so profoundly that our older two children don't desire to have anything to do with the church, although they maintain their relationship with God. As a pastor's kid myself, I know all too well the devastation of church hurt on pastors' families. Throughout that entire time, my sole focus was on keeping my family safe.

Through that entire ordeal, I wore a mask. I was hurting deeply, yet I held my head high and smiled through it all. It's never easy to see your loved ones being hurt. But it's tough when the hurt is inflicted by people with whom you thought you had a good relationship. It's never easy feeling betrayed and stabbed in the back by those who, at some point, smiled in your face and provided you with hugs that felt genuine. I wanted to lash out at those whom I thought betrayed, not only my husband but my children and me. At the same time, however, I felt that I needed to use that energy to be strong for and comfort my family.

My husband and children could cry on my shoulder or vent about what had happened, but I kept it all in. I learned at a very early age never to get too close to people in the church because, ultimately, they would hurt you. I learned later that this is not true of everyone in the church; however, I still felt I needed to shield myself by not blurring the lines with church members, and it is a coping mechanism that I still use today. I sincerely try to treat everyone the same and am sure not to make "friends" with church members. It can be a very lonely place to be yet safe.

When the ordeal happened at the church and my husband, with God's leading, decided to resign, I knew that this might put him in a tailspin of depression. While I had my own feelings to deal with about the situation, I couldn't deal with them because I was anxious about what this decision might do to him. I knew that we were in for a rough road ahead. Although my faith was and is very strong, I was nervous about what the future held for our family.

Externally, I appeared to have dealt with the situation well. I moved along with life appearing to have never missed a beat. Several people would ask me, "How are you staying so strong and poised through this?" My answer, "only God." While it was factual that God was keeping me, I still felt pain deep down inside. I kept pushing it down and wearing the mask. I don't think I honestly realized how much the turmoil affected me until one day recently. I received a message on Facebook Messenger from one of the former members with whom my children and I, especially my oldest daughter, had been very close. She messaged me about an accomplishment of one of our children that I posted about on Facebook. As I read the message, something rose in me that I didn't realize existed. She was one with whom I had become close who had turned her back on our family.

I didn't realize that there was pain with which I had not dealt. Here was one, whom I once thought of as a Godly person, whom I saw stand with liars and thieves over the man of God. At that moment, as I read the message and thought to myself, how dare you, one who hurt my children so deeply, have anything to say about them, I realized that I had bottled emotions that I hadn't released. I have never been one to hold a grudge, and I likely would have let it go had this person not been one who hurt my children. Even as I type this, I feel myself becoming overwhelmed with emotion because I continue to repress it and wear the mask. I never responded to the message for fear of what might have come out. However, as a woman of God, I should have let her know that she offended my children and me. I should have, in a tactful way, let her know how deeply she hurt us, but instead, I tucked it away and continued wearing the mask.

I'm not sure what it will take for me to eradicate the mask. In some ways, I suppose writing this book is one way for me to work toward being more vulnerable. I truly believe that vulnerability is necessary for healing and ministering to others. I will definitely need to continue going before the Lord to help me to garner the strength in Him to take off the mask. Like everything in life, it is a process that won't happen overnight, but with persistence and God's leading, it will happen.

6 TURNING THE SCREAM INSIDE OUT: CARING FOR ME TOO

I Need Me

Somewhere along this journey, I began to feel the need to focus on myself. This is very difficult for me because my natural inclination is toward others, especially those with whom I have the closest relationships. I thought that focusing on my spiritual, mental, and physical well-being meant that I was selfish. Focusing on myself is very difficult because I feel that I am just not wired that way. When engaging in an encounter, even with total strangers, I am generally more concerned with their wellbeing than my own. I'm not sure why.

I am the type of person who will put others' needs before my own. I had gotten into the habit of allowing others into my space when I needed the space all to myself. In other words, I needed me! My husband would always try to encourage me when I needed "me time" to let him and the kids know so they could give me space. Of course, that didn't work. I would never turn away my husband or my children if they needed me. Many days, as soon as I walked in the door, I would get bombarded with each one needing something from me. Don't get me wrong. I loved that everyone felt that they could come to me about anything and that they seemed to miss me. I was happy to engage them, but at least let me get in, take off my coat, get comfortable and relax, relate, release a little after a long day at work.

I tried to think of creative ways to get some "me time." Sometimes, I would even go into the bathroom just to be left alone. I wouldn't be using it, just pretending and thinking, "No one will bother me here." Wrong! My children would ultimately come looking for me. I could hear them in my room outside of the bathroom door waiting for me. After a while, one would finally say, "Mom, what are you doing? How long you gonna be?" I know lots of moms can relate to this scenario. ☺

It's funny to think about, but also sad. It's unfortunate because the more I didn't take the time to take a moment and breathe, the more stressed I became. I was good for telling others to "take care of yourself because if you don't take care of yourself first, you can't take care of others who are depending on you." I would use the familiar analogy of putting the oxygen mask on yourself before assisting others in the case of an emergency while in flight. How many times have I dished that advice and not taken heed to it myself? Numerous times! I saw a bumper sticker one day on which the words were written, "Take my advice. I don't use it anyway." Oh, how I can relate to that! I'm sure many who will read this can relate, too. There came the point in my life when I realized that *I need me*.

Needing me meant that sometimes I couldn't be available to everyone else without being available for me first. It meant that I would need to say to my husband and children, "Not right now. I'm taking time for myself." Those were the most difficult eight words ever! Even as I write this, I have been talking about getting away for a self-retreat. I have literally been TALKING about it for years! To this day, I still haven't done it. Although I haven't yet accomplished the goal, I at least went from talking about it to writing it down on my vision board. After writing it on my vision board, I set a date to do it the days leading into my 50th birthday. I did go so far as to attempt to make the reservation at the retreat center that I wanted to visit; however, it was closed for a winter/holiday break. When that didn't work, I set a new goal, and I am determined to make it happen.

At the ripe, young age of 50 years, I have finally come to realize that needing me is not a crime. It's okay to need "me time" and to take it! It's okay to take a trip by myself. A part of turning the scream inside out is for me to allow myself the time and space to constructively and helpfully scream outwardly.

Permitting Myself to Scream

I finally permitted myself to scream. There were times that I felt the need always to wear a happy mask regardless of how I felt inside. I believed that it was expected of me not outwardly to show that I was actually in a bad mood. I also have always tried to be careful to spare others of the times that I might be in a bad mood. But why was I trying so hard to put up this façade of a perfect image? What was I trying to prove, and to whom? It came to me that sometimes, people need to see when you're in a bad mood so they can connect with your humanness. I thought that since my husband experienced mood swings due to depression, I needed to be the constant source of "upbeatness" in the house. But that simply was and is not true. When you take off the mask and allow others to see that you too need comfort rather than be the comforter; you too need a listening ear rather than always being the listener; you too need them to sometimes suppress their bad mood so you can give way to yours, deal with it and move on, then you can truly walk in the fulness of all that you are.

I realized that sometimes, just like I was present for my family, I needed to allow them the space to be present for me, too. In wearing the mask of always obliging others, being in a good mood, comforting others, I wasn't allowing them to see that I need them too. I had to permit myself to need them. It's not that they weren't there for me to begin with, but I needed to recognize that it's not all about me. There was a certain level of self-righteousness involved in exuding pseudo-perfection. I needed to get a grip, remove the mask, and allow myself to *be.*

I Can't Take that Trip

There were times that when my husband was in a deep depression, I found myself going there with him. It is very difficult to be in a marriage- that is, to be one with another human being and not take on their pain. When you truly love someone, you want to use all of your might to take away any pain in which they may find themselves. I would find myself not only becoming depressed because of the pain in which my husband found himself, but depressed because I could not figure out how to snap him out of it. So, there I would be, buckled up and riding shotgun and taking a trip to depression with him.

I'm not sure at what point I decided that I could no longer take these trips. Unlike him, I didn't have a therapist. I know, I chose not to, so that's on me. But at the time, I didn't have someone- a human being, with whom to talk about these trips. Even so, I realized that if I kept buckling in for these rides, at some point, I wouldn't be able to release the belt. I was beginning to spiral downward inwardly, and I couldn't allow that to happen. If I crashed, the entire household would crash. My husband needed me. My children needed me. I needed me.

Once I decided not to take the trip with my husband to depression, I then had to develop specific strategies to depart from the familiar and ride solo during those episodes. When the depression caused mood swings, and I found myself about to buckle in, I'd say to myself, "Nope, I cannot take that trip." Once I consciously decided not to take the trip, I would then intentionally find ways to take my own journeys so as not to lose my happy place. I began to not only give him his personal space to work through the episode, but I would also take my personal space as well. I would listen to music or watch one of my favorite old shows that my husband teases me about watching. I would find ways to stay positive. I realized that although we are one, and I love him with all my heart, I didn't have to take every depressive trip with him, and I didn't have to feel bad about not taking the trip. It didn't mean that I loved him less or didn't want to be with him. It just meant that my mental well-being was important, too. In those moments, I needed to take care of myself by taking a different trip, and that's okay.

Don't Take it Personal

Another way that I have turned the scream inside out is by not taking my husband's episodes of depression (which at this point have become fewer and fewer) personally. I mentioned earlier how when we were first married, and before I understood that he suffered from depression, I would take the mood swings personally. I realized that it was not about me. Of course, there were times that something I did or said might have made him angry and vice versa. That's to be expected in any relationship. But not every mood swing was about something that I said or did.

Another way that I began to care for myself was to develop relationships with other like-minded women intentionally. Although I attended an all-female public high school and joined a sorority in college, I always found it difficult to relate to other females. As a young child, most of my associates were male. I felt that females tended to keep up a lot of unnecessary drama, and I don't do drama.

However, as a mature woman, I realize how important it is to fellowship with other women. I began getting involved in groups of professional or Christian women. I would schedule lunch or dinner outings with sister-friends regularly, and even when things came up and we had to cancel, I was determined to reschedule until we made the meeting happen.

Since I have always had difficulty connecting with other women, I am also more introverted when I am around other women. I am trying to develop ways of breaking out of that and forcing myself to engage in ways that I am not accustomed to. Creating outlets for one's self is an essential step toward self-care and preservation. I have realized that being intentional about designing these outlets is a must. I have not perfected it yet, but

I'm trying. One of my relatively recent sister-friends teaches me the art of doing nice things for yourself and doing them big! She may not realize that she's teaching me, but I'm watching her and gleaning. One day, perhaps I'll put it into play on a grand scale, but for now, as my first-born says, I'll start with baby steps.

It's good to know that there are others in the human realm to whom I can turn for support, encouragement, love, a listening ear, etc., but there's truly no one to whom I can turn like my God. Faith plays such an integral role in how we have been able to manage throughout the years. As intentional as I have been developing relationships with other like-minded women, I am even more intentional about growing a deeper faith. I want to make sure that my heart is connected to the heart of God so that it beats in sync with my provider, deliverer, redeemer, and sustainer!

7 SCREAMING BY FAITH

Screaming by Faith- The Proverbs 31:10-31 Dilemma

Proverbs 31:10-31 is one of the most utilized scriptures to show what a woman should do and be for her family and the Kingdom of God. The poem in these verses describes a woman who literally is everything to and does everything for her family. The following is the New International Version (NIV) of the text:

Epilogue: The Wife of Noble Character

10 A wife of noble character who can find?
   She is worth far more than rubies.
11 Her husband has full confidence in her
   and lacks nothing of value.
12 She brings him good, not harm,
   all the days of her life.
13 She selects wool and flax
   and works with eager hands.
14 She is like the merchant ships,
   bringing her food from afar.
15 She gets up while it is still night;

she provides food for her family

and portions for her female servants.

16 She considers a field and buys it;

out of her earnings she plants a vineyard.

17 She sets about her work vigorously;

her arms are strong for her tasks.

18 She sees that her trading is profitable,

and her lamp does not go out at night.

19 In her hand she holds the distaff

and grasps the spindle with her fingers.

20 She opens her arms to the poor

and extends her hands to the needy.

21 When it snows, she has no fear for her household;

for all of them are clothed in scarlet.

22 She makes coverings for her bed;

she is clothed in fine linen and purple.

23 Her husband is respected at the city gate,

where he takes his seat among the elders of the land.

24 She makes linen garments and sells them,

and supplies the merchants with sashes.

25 She is clothed with strength and dignity;

she can laugh at the days to come.

26 She speaks with wisdom,

and faithful instruction is on her tongue.

27 She watches over the affairs of her household

and does not eat the bread of idleness.

28 Her children arise and call her blessed;

her husband also, and he praises her:

29 "Many women do noble things,

but you surpass them all."

30 Charm is deceptive, and beauty is fleeting;

but a woman who fears the Lord is to be praised.

31 Honor her for all that her hands have done,

and let her works bring her praise at the city gate.

The poem speaks of the many gifts and talents that a man who finds a wife should have. It is also important to note that this advice was from a mother to her son, a king. The poem displays the characteristics of a good wife and the many splendid gifts she brings to her family and community, including hard work and provision for her household, being a business and landowner, making provisions for the needy, and making clothing to shield her husband and children from the harsh elements of winter. I wonder if when Ashford and Simpson penned the lyrics of the song first made famous by Chaka Khan, then Whitney Houston, "I'm Every Woman," they had read this scripture. The lyrics state, "I'm every woman, it's all in me. Anything you want done, Baby, I do it naturally."

Both the poem in Proverbs and the song give the notion that good women worthy of a man's choosing can do it all. While, on the one hand, it's good for women to know that they can possess these qualities, it's dangerous for them to feel like they must possess them all and kill themselves, striving to be everything to everyone to the neglect of themselves. Unfortunately, many women in the Christian community, in particular, take the words of the poem to literally mean that a good Christian woman should do all of these things and not expect help from her husband as he sits at the gate chillin' with his homies, her children watch and offer no assistance, and she should be ok with that. The Proverb is not meant for women to take literally that they are supposed to do all of these things. Instead, it suggests that these are things that a woman could accomplish, and she should not be held back from them. The most important thing that women should get from the poem is that "…a woman who fears the Lord is to be praised."

I believe that women often try so hard to be the woman described in the Proverbs 31 poem that they miss the part about fearing the Lord. A woman who reverences the Lord will seek the Lord's guidance about how to live her life in the context of her marriage and family. Moreover, she will not neglect her temple, which is the Holy Spirit's dwelling place, by doing too much and not requiring the same of her family.

I am fortunate to have a husband who works hard for our family and shares equally in work at home. Our faith helps us to understand that not only are we a team, but we are on the same team in Christ. We are both put here together on purpose and to glorify our Savior, Jesus the Christ. Our shared faith and ministry has enabled us to confront and deal with all of the challenges that life has thrown our way since we came together over 26 years ago. We both are keenly aware that God truly put us together, and therefore, we will allow nothing or no one to break us apart.

I am blessed that although I do work hard to help support our family, I don't have to do it alone. Through it all, my husband and I are there for each other, and our faith gives us the strength and the tools we need to keep pushing when the world would say give up and keep holding on when the world would say let go. I may not possess all of the skills described of the woman in Proverbs 31, but my husband and children still rise up and call me blessed because I fear the Lord, and I trust Him with everything that concerns me.

Quiet Time with God

One of the practices that I have begun to engage in is quiet time with God. This came about as a result of my prayer with God one day. I wanted to be more deliberate about carving out time with God, where I was not only praying to God, but I was listening for instruction from Him. One day, as I got into my car to head to work, I heard the Holy Spirit say, "don't turn on any music." Now, those who know me and know how much music means to me know how difficult it was for me to ride on my 45-minute to one-hour commute to work in complete silence!

The first day was a struggle, but I was obedient to the Spirit. I wondered why I was being directed to turn off the music. After all, my commute to work was my time to turn on gospel music and worship. At first, I couldn't understand why the Spirit wouldn't want me to engage in my usual worship on my way to work. But in the silence, the Spirit spoke to me and said, 1) worship is not only about listening to gospel music to get your shout on! 2) worship is about your heart connecting with mine, and sometimes you're so into the rhythm of the music or the song lyrics that you miss what I'm trying to say to you! Whew! That part- as Jada Pinkett-Smith would say. It was then that I realized that God was trying to speak to me directly, but the music was too loud for me to hear Him!

I have kept this practice going now over the last several months. Before, I couldn't wait to get in the car and program my music for the trip. Now, I can't wait to get in the car and experience God's presence in our "we-time" together. It is like a breath of fresh air! Admittedly, there are times in the silence when my mind wanders, but without the loud music to cover up His voice, the Spirit gets me back on track quickly! This is the space where God is continuously working on me and preparing me for the plans He has for me.

I realize that in caring for myself and preparing to remove the mask, it's vital for me to grow closer and closer to my creator, redeemer, sustainer, and healer. I know that it is only the triune God who has sustained me amid life's challenges, and it is my Lord and Savior who will continue to see me through.

Faith and Therapy are not Mutually Exclusive

Often, Christians make the mistake of thinking that seeing a therapist means operating in a lack of faith- that you can't have faith and therapy at the same time. This is an unfortunate stance because I believe that God can and will lead us to those whom He has gifted in the area of therapy to help walk us through the process of discovering the root causes of our wounds so that we can truly heal.

I truly believe that God led my husband to his first therapist and his current therapist, both of whom have assisted in helping him to heal. Some spouses may feel that they are inadequate to assist their other half if he or she needs to seek a therapist to get help. But the most important thing for a spouse who cares for one who deals with depression is to support them by encouraging them to seek therapy and to make them feel comfortable in doing so. Also, let them know that their concerns matter, even if they don't seem like such a big deal to you. Seeking therapy does not indicate a lack of faith, and not seeking therapy doesn't demonstrate abundant faith. God created humankind with different abilities that all can be used in His service. Seek God in all of it and watch Him work!

8 LOVE IS THE CURE

Love Is the Cure

1 Corinthians 13:1-8

"If I speak in the tongues of men or of angels, but do not have love, I am only a resounding gong or a clanging cymbal. **2** If I have the gift of prophecy and can fathom all mysteries and all knowledge, and if I have a faith that can move mountains, but do not have love, I am nothing. **3** If I give all I possess to the poor and give over my body to hardship that I may boast, but do not have love, I gain nothing.

4 Love is patient, love is kind. It does not envy, it does not boast, it is not proud. 5 It does not dishonor others, it is not self-seeking, It Is not easily angered, it keeps no record of wrongs. 6 Love does not delight in evil but rejoices with the truth. 7 It always protects, always trusts, always hopes, always perseveres. 8 Love never fails."

My husband would often ask me why I choose to stay in our marriage, and the answer is quite simple- because I genuinely love him. It's not the superficial- I love you if, but just- I love you-period. As I mentioned in the previous chapter, the most important aspect or characteristic of a Proverbs 31 woman is that she fears the Lord. My fear, respect, adoration, worship, and love of God are what encumbers me to love my husband through everything. Not only that, the recognition that I, too, am a flawed individual and the fact that he also loves me through my flaws enables me to return that kind of love.

Love is Patient and Kind

Because my love for my husband is agape, i.e., I love you, rather than an Eros kind of love, i.e., I love you if, it gives me the strength to exercise patience and kindness rather than impatience and hostility. A person who goes through severe depression needs a balance of patience and compassion in the absence of enabling. I mean that the person needs to feel loved and safe to combat the depression in the way that best fits him or her. Simultaneously, they do not need to be allowed to wallow in the pit of depression. They need to be allowed a moment to acknowledge that they are having a bout of depression but then need that push that says, "Ok, enough of that. It's time for you to push through to the other side and not permit the depression to take over." People who suffer from depression need that extra boost of confidence that they are loved despite what they might endure while in a depressed state.

Love Does Not Dishonor Others

There are times when it's easy for those of us who don't suffer from depression to simply not get it. We don't understand why specific triggers cause our loved ones to go into a depressed state. We don't know why they seem to let certain things and even particular people get to them. We just don't understand, and in our lack of understanding, we sometimes give off the sense that what they're going through is petty and doesn't matter. But it does matter, and we need to honor and empathize with how they feel. Empathy is "the action of understanding, being aware of, being sensitive to, and vicariously experiencing the feelings, thoughts, and experience of another of either the past or present without having the feelings, thoughts, and experience fully communicated in an objectively explicit manner."[15] We don't have to have experienced what the depressed person has, but we need to acknowledge that they did and that what they are enduring matters.

Love is Not Self-Seeking

If you think it's all about you, think again. When you are a caregiver to a person dealing with depression, it's essential to know that there are days that their depression will undoubtedly affect you. There will even be days when you want to throw in the towel because it's more than you can bear. But hold on; don't let go because as frustrated as you might get, remember that the person dealing with the depression is that much more frustrated. I don't entirely know what it feels like to have days where you can't muster up the strength to do anything except keep your head buried under the covers. I don't know what it feels like to cry for hours on end and not know how to stop. In those moments, I can't deal with how they affect me- I can do that later, but in those

---

[15] Merriam-Webster Dictionary for Iphone 2019.

moments, a loved one needs a hug, a shoulder to cry on, or maybe even some space to figure it all out themselves.

Love is Not Easily Angered and Keeps no Record of Wrongs

Whew! What a mouth full! In marriage, it's easy to fall into being easily angered because we are keeping track of our spouse's wrongs. However, when it comes to our iniquities, we seem to have "selective amnesia," meaning we forget the part we may have played in the conflict. One of the absolute worse things a person can do to their spouse is to throw up past grievances in their face constantly. Doing this is a fast track to marital breakdown. It's also a fast track to forgetting what brought you together in the first place.

As I stated above, when caring for one who battles depression, it's easy to become frustrated and keep track of all the wrongs, and then use them as an excuse to bail on the relationship. However, as long as the relationship is not abusive (neither physical nor verbal), exercising true love will enable you to keep track of the rights while working through the wrongs together. This may not be an easy task, but true love will prove that it's worth the effort.

Love does not delight in evil but rejoices with the truth

In a marriage or any relationship, for that matter, there may be times where one person does or says things to hurt the other, which causes the one who is hurt to desire ill will toward the other. There are times that we may want to see the one who broke our hearts to be miserable, especially if he or she left us for someone else. But love requires the opposite. Love requires that we hope for the good, even for those who have mistreated and done us wrong. It doesn't require that we be a doormat, however.

In marriage, we must remember that our spouse is the other half of us, so when we desire ill will for that person, we too want it for ourselves. While I have never personally experienced a time where I had ill will toward my spouse, even in his depressed state, there may be someone reading this who has had those thoughts. I would encourage those people to love themselves enough to pray for God to take captive any thoughts of ill will toward their spouse.

It always protects, always trusts, always hopes, always perseveres. Love never fails!

Love always protects- it covers or shields from exposure, injury, damage, or destruction. It maintains the status or integrity of something or someone.[16] My love for my husband is such that I desire to protect him. It is crucial for me to be a shoulder to cry on, his "voice of reason," and shield him from his triggers to the best of my ability. It is also crucial that I supported him in his decision to seek professional therapy. Encouraging him to release his fears to God and seek the help he needed would protect him through not only helping him to identify his triggers and the types of events that would bring about the triggers but also by providing him with tools that would allow him to combat bouts of depression.

Love always trusts- relies on the character, ability, strength, or truth of someone or something. One of the most notable attributes of my husband is his character. I find his integrity and honesty refreshing in a world where fakeness and hypocrisy are the norms. Whether or not he is in a depressive state, he remains the same concerning having a pure heart. It is that truth about him and my trust in God that helps me to always see this truth in him

---

[16] Meriam-Webster Dictionary for Iphone 6S, 2019.

clearly. No matter how often he finds himself in a state of depression, he remains faithful to God, his family, and those whom he serves as pastor, and other roles as well. Over our 25 years together, I have relied on who God is to overcome the stress that often comes with depression. It is in God, who is love, that we can have the strength to endure the rough times so that the good times are brighter than we might expect.

Love always hopes- cherishes a desire with anticipation; wants something to happen or be true. I always believed in the hope that one day, my husband would be healed of depression. I have spent many years praying for him to be able to find joy within. I have seen his increased ability to move out of depressive episodes. I've noticed that there are many more days between bouts of depression than there used to be. With each passing day, he is healing and able to cope more than the day before. I have come to realize that healing doesn't always come in a miraculous, microwave, rapid manner, but tiny bits of healing that come with the dawning of each new day over 25+ years still counts.

I am grateful that my God gives me hope every day that by His stripes, my husband is healed. In the natural, it may not look like complete healing, but by faith, I believe God that it is done. The hope of complete healing started with recognizing that healing was needed and progressed with the desire to put in the work required to move closer to the complete healing that God desires. Without hope, healing would not have been possible because healing requires faith on some level. It is by faith that we are made whole.

Love always perseveres- persists in a state, enterprise, or undertaking in spite of counterinfluences, opposition, or discouragement.[17] Depression can be thought of as a counterinfluence, opposition, or discouragement. Depression can cause a person to push against the very ones who care about them the most and vice versa. But love always perseveres- it

---

[17] Meriam-Webster Dictionary for Iphone 6S, 2019

pushes against the depression and drives through the struggle. Even in the darkest moments, love says, "I've got you. It's difficult, the load is heavy, the distance is far, but together, we will carry the load clear across the finish line!" Perseverance is not about arriving at a destination quickly; rather, it's about arriving at the destination- period.

All marriages, even in the absence of depression or some other chronic illness, require perseverance to get through some rough patches. Perseverance may look different on each person. For one, it may look like quiet patience with each step- like they are wearing the best walking shoe ever created. For another, it may look like strain and pain with each step, like they are wearing shoes a size too small, yet they are still stepping. Just because your step looks different than someone else's doesn't mean that you're not persevering. It just means that your stride is different, but you will still reach the desired destination as long as you keep stepping!

Love never fails- it never loses strength or weakens; it never fades or dies away; it never stops functioning. Love is a continuous state of being. It's not something you do until the kids leave the house. It's not something that is done on the condition of something else. Love just is! When we see love as a state of being rather than a superficial emotion, we become better equipped to live out a love that never fails despite its circumstances.

9 THE SHOE ON THE OTHER FOOT

The Shoe on the Other Foot

One night recently, my husband and I were returning from a worship service we attended and decided to stop and get a bite to eat. Around that time, I was having some difficulty with my job. I was encountering some depression myself because I no longer found the job to be fulfilling. Moreover, I had already published my first book, *Living the Word Beyond Sunday Morning: Practical Ways to Live God's Word and Make an Impact for God's Kingdom*, and a workbook to go with it. On top of that, I also developed a workshop of the same title (minus the subtitle). I was being fulfilled by creating those items, and I have more books to write (including this one!). I had gotten to a place where I wanted to spend all of my time writing and creating for the Kingdom, but my bills told me not to quit my day job, which is paying the college tuition for all three of my children!

I was in a fog and a deep depression because it was starting to impact my job performance. I strive for excellence in all that I do. I don't necessarily strive for perfection (getting everything 100% correct 100% of the time), but excellence (striving toward perfection or providing high-quality work) is a must! I began to feel low about myself and my abilities. It got so bad that I would awaken in the morning with all kinds of anxieties around going to work. I was having heart palpitations at the thought of going into the office. Although at this point, I had been working with my supervisor for nearly five years, I still felt inadequate because while I had been a research project manager for more than 20 years, I had never managed the type of research in which she was engaged. Furthermore, there was more of a need for me to become better acquainted with data management software- something that, in the past, I had been able to hire a data manager to do.

I am facing what many people face toward the end of a career- difficulty changing with the times. I know that I need to update my project management skills, but at the same time, I'm not very motivated to do so. I am in pre-retirement mode, just passing the time until I can officially retire in 4 years and receive full benefits. There's a part of me that wishes I were there already and I could spend all of my time doing ministry-related activities.

As I purged myself to my husband that night, I began to see that the shoe was now on the other foot. Unlike before, providing the shoulder for him to cry on, I was now crying on his. It occurred to me that in the past, I didn't cry on his shoulder much because I was afraid that it might plunge him into a depression. But that night, I wasn't at all afraid that something I said might depress him. As I told him about all of my angst and the tears began to roll, he was able to pull me out of the pit of depression. He did so by reminding me of why I took the job in the first place. He reminded me that I was excited about the challenge of learning new information and that I wanted to add clinical research to my resume.

This discussion helped me change my perspective and view my work as an exciting challenge rather than a chore. Moreover, in my quiet time with God, He reminded me that He put me there on purpose. You see, I was facing a lay-off and had three months to find employment within the university and maintain my benefits at the same level. When I initially saw the job posted, I did not plan to apply for it because it was two pay grades below my current grade, and I refused to take a pay cut. But then I received an e-mail from human resources encouraging me to apply for the job. My goal was to use it as a practice interview since it had been many years since I had to interview for a job. During the interview, I was very straightforward that the pay grade was too low. By the end of the interview, my now supervisor was contacting human resources about how she could increase the pay grade to hire me. That was nobody but God! He reminded me that my purpose there was much bigger than the job itself- I was placed there on purpose and for God's purpose!

My husband had reminded me that I should not accept defeat. This was something that I repeatedly told him, and now he had to say it to me. I can't tell you how good it felt at that moment to switch shoes with him. I know that sounds strange, and no, I would never desire to have the kind of depression with which he is challenged. But it felt good to be the one to unload for a change. I didn't realize how freeing it could be!

But I also learned something else at that moment. My husband, through years of prayer and therapy, was getting mentally stronger. He is a different man today than he was some 25 years ago when we first met, and I am a different woman. He is much more patient, and bouts of depression are few and far between. He now has tools to understand what triggers his depression and how to overcome them. I no longer feel like I'm walking on eggshells, wondering how I might find him when I arrive home in the evenings. *He* is stronger; therefore, *we* are stronger! We are one! Yes, there have been challenges over the years, but there's nothing that we can't face and tackle together with our God.

Reconnection

One of the best pieces of pre-marital advice that my husband and I received was from my former supervisor when I was employed at Johns Hopkins University School of Public Health. She told us that when we begin to have children, to keep the connection between us strong because one day, the children will grow up and leave, and we will need to be able to connect on more than just the children. Fast forward 24+ years, she couldn't have been more accurate. During the years of raising our children, most of our conversations were about them and, if not them, the church.

I don't think I realized how much our conversations focused on church and the children until we recently became empty-nesters. At first, it was strange for us to have the house all to ourselves, but we quickly became adjusted to having just us. We decided to take a brief get-a-way trip, and on that trip, it felt like old times. We talked about many things, but mainly our future goals and not much about the children or the church. It was a wonderful experience for both of us, reconnecting on many levels, and just enjoying each other's company. We vowed that we would be more intentional about making time each day to talk and stay connected on a deep level.

During our trip, I opened up to my husband about many things that I went through, much of which is written in this book. That's something that I didn't dare to discuss with him before, but now I feel comfortable to discuss. It was so freeing and therapeutic for me and a reminder that he can be there for me emotionally, just as I have been for him over the years. I was also reminded that when our relationship first started, it was with him talking me through the pain I experienced in my previous break-up. I see that a lot of what I tried to protect him from, I didn't need to protect him. Rather than tip-toeing around certain things, we could have just talked about them like we did before marriage. I am so glad that we are now in this place where we are both committed to keeping our bond solid and intentional about putting in the time needed with each other to make sure that happens consistently.

The Scream Without

I no longer feel like I have to scream within because I can be open and honest without fear of a bout of depression coming on as a result. I am grateful to God for how He has operated in our lives throughout the years and thankful to my husband for recognizing that he needed additional help and not letting stigma get in the way of that. It wasn't easy initially, but he made up his mind that he wanted to get better for himself and our family. I want to encourage anyone reading this who may face similar challenges that there's no challenge too great for our God. Prayer and therapy are not mutually exclusive- both are imperative for handling depression in the faith community. Now that you have my story, my scream within can now be a scream without- without fear, without condemnation, without ridicule, without embarrassment. To God be the glory!

ABOUT THE AUTHOR

Reverend Benita Weathers is the owner and CEO of BL Weathers LLC, a multifaceted consulting business that facilitates the client's ability to *"Discover what becomes you!"* She is an ordained preacher, author, teacher, certified life coach, podcaster, and editor.

Rev. Weathers is interested in the holistic health of individuals - spiritual, mental, and physical. With training in divinity, public health, and biology, she is uniquely equipped to provide strategic and practical means by which individuals can achieve wholeness in their lives. She is especially interested in removing the stigma in the church and African American communities regarding mental health and assisting individuals over the age of 40 to discover (or rediscover) what's already inside them and utilize those gifts toward a life that is fulfilling.

Rev. Weathers is the author of *Living the Word Beyond Sunday Morning: Practical Ways to Live God's Word and Make an Impact for God's Kingdom* Bible study guide and self-workbook, and has been a featured speaker at workshop trainings, conferences, and worship services. She is the mother of three adult children, a Senior Research Project Manager at the University of Pennsylvania, and a member of Alpha Kappa Alpha Sorority, Inc.

FB: @RevBenitaWeathers

Instagram: @benita_weathers

Twitter: @BenitaWeathers

Hashtags: #RevBLWeathersinspirations #livingthewordbeyondsundaymorning #ltwbsm #benitaweathers

Website: www.benitaweathers.com

www.gloriousworkspublishing.com

www.ingramcontent.com/pod-product-compliance
Lightning Source LLC
Chambersburg PA
CBHW031523270326
41930CB00006B/509